WHY CATS PAINT

A theory of feline aesthetics

POCKET EDITION

Burton Silver

Heather Busch

TEN SPEED PRESS
Berkeley | Toronto

10

TEN SPEED PRESS
P.O. Box 7123
Berkeley, California 94707
www.tenspeed.com

Distributed in Australia by Simon & Schuster Australia, in Canada by Ten Speed Press Canada, in New Zealand by Southern Publishers Group, in South Africa by Real Books, and in the United Kingdom and Europe by Publishers Group UK.

Library of Congress Cataloging-in-publication data on file with the publisher.

ISBN-13: 978-1-58008-793-3

ISBN-10: 1-58008-793-0

RIGHT: Mindle and Moitle (left), painting *Swinging Swallows*, 1994. Scented acrylic on card, 48 x 65 cm. Private collection.

PAGE 1: Misty painting *A Little Lavish Leaping*, 1993.

PAGE 2: *Beam Me Up*, 1982. Acrylic on yellow card, 48 x 68 cm. F. Norbert Collection.

First printing, 2006.

Printed in China.

1 2 3 4 5 6 7 8 9 10 — 10 09 08 07 06

FOREWORD

My late husband, Dr. Arthur Mann, has been credited with the discovery of representational marking by domestic cats, but I don't think he'd mind me telling you that he was given crucial guidance by a couple of three-year-olds—one a beautiful ginger tom called Orangello, the other an equally beautiful little girl called Francesca.

In 1982, Arthur was staying with Orangello's owners, the Norberts, in order to study their cat's prolific marking behavior as part of his thesis on feline territorial demarcation activity. The walls of the big studio were festooned with Orangello's colorful works, each one carefully labelled as to where and when it was

---

LEFT: Orangello pauses during an invertist painting of dahlias to observe a parrot. While Orangello did not chase the parrot, he was obviously put off by its presence and later destroyed the work with obliterative lines. This strongly suggests the painting was a mood piece rather than a representational work.

done, the medium used, the time taken, and the ratio of verticals to horizontals. But after five months, he was no closer to any coherent explanation.

It was the Norberts' three-year-old daughter who broke the code. Lying on the floor one afternoon, sucking her bottle and looking back over her head, she pointed at a painting and said, "Moo-cow!" And, "That moo too!" Later in the day, when she walked back in, Arthur playfully asked her to point out the moo-cows again. At first Francesca just stared blankly, but then, twisting her head round to look at the pictures upside down, she quickly identified them both. Intrigued, Arthur tried doing the same and was amazed to find crude but recognizable images of familiar objects in the house, like the large wooden cow that was used as a door stop. Orangello was painting real things upside down!

At last, cat painting could cease to be dismissed as some kind of instinctive territorial marking behavior and begin to be seen as a preplanned communication. Just what that communication is and what the motivation behind it might be can still only be guessed at. Had someone taken over my husband's research when he died, I feel certain we would know a lot more than we do today. But perhaps Orangello provided us with a hint in his last major work, Beam Me Up (see frontispiece), which he painted the day after Francesca's little toy Scottie dog was irretrievably lost down an old well. To us, it is a lyrical and well-balanced work, suggestive perhaps of flowers on a spring day or an after-banquet fluttering of peacock feathers, but to Francesca, who lost no time in looking at it upside down, it revealed the unmistakable pointy ears and snub nose of her beloved Scottie.

Nora Mann

PREFACE

Can you see the cat's tail? We so seldom consider the feline origins of the question mark that this old written riddle still puzzles children and adults the world over. The classical curled-over tail of the curious cat is still found in most of our written texts as the symbol used to denote a question. It is our hope that by exploring the signs a small number of domestic cats continue to make today, we may rekindle an interest in their unique way of perceiving the world and perhaps derive valuable insights from it.

While theories on the aesthetics of nonprimate signing are hardly new, we are aware that the great popularity of the domestic cat as a pet means any attempt to describe their marks as art carries with it certain dangers. The growing commercial value of cat art has, for example, led not only to some misguided breeding programs (notably with Persians in Australia), but also to a few cases, thankfully rare, where cats have been

trained to create art works for reward.

It is our belief that we must suppress our desire to see cats confirming our perceptions and values through their art, and rather than attempting to determine the direction of their aesthetic development on our terms, we must allow those few cats who paint to develop their own special potential. Only in this way can we be certain they will be able to communicate their unique, undiluted view of the world and perhaps provide us with the clues we need to ensure the survival and future well-being of all species—provided, of course, we can trust them to tell us the truth.

Burton Silver and Heather Busch,
Wellington, 2006

INTRODUCTION

The pictures you see below are from a videotape of a nameless male cat painting on a television program in Russia in 1978. It was sent to us by a colleague in Moscow and was our first clear evidence that cats can make intentional marks of an aesthetic nature. In the video, the cat begins by staring at the two canvases taped to the wall for several minutes before stepping up to one of the saucers at their base and carefully brushing his paw pads lightly over the surface

of the thick paint it contains. Then, perfectly balanced on his hind legs, he very deliberately reaches up and, holding his front paws together, makes two little black dots high up on the canvas. Dropping back down, he sits and contemplates his handiwork for a while before studiously collecting more paint and turning the dots into two angular smears. He carefully repeats this motif on the other side of the canvas, then takes another, even longer break to survey his progress. Then, as if suddenly inspired, he attacks the canvas with deft little flicks and completes a series of three white crosses in a neat row, and as if to say that's what he meant to do all along, he repeats the crosses on the next canvas. Finally, with scarcely a glance at what he's done, he nonchalantly

walks outside to wash his paws. The whole operation lasts only a few minutes, but it's performed with such casual grace it appears as if nothing unusual has occurred at all.

Many people have similar feelings the first time they watch a cat painting. It seems such a perfectly natural thing for the cat to be doing that not until later do they think to examine the cat's motivation—and when they do, the questions come tumbling out. Is it trying to represent something, an object maybe or perhaps an emotional state, and why? Could it be trying to communicate with us or another cat, or is painting a way of exploring its inner feelings? Do some cats actually have an aesthetic sense or is their "art" simply a form of territorial marking behavior, as many biologists believe? We are much closer to finding the answers to these questions today than we were when we first saw that videotape twenty-eight years ago. A great deal has been discovered about cat painting over the intervening years, and we hope that sharing some of this knowledge with you now may give you insights that could help find solutions to the many mysteries that still remain—grinning down at us out of the branches above.

BELOW & PAGES 12–13: This male Birman appeared on a Russian television program in 1978. Little is known about Russian cat painting generally and nothing is known about this cat in particular, except that the remarkable symmetry of its designs show it to be a highly advanced painter.

HISTORICAL

In 1990, a dramatic discovery was made by an Australian archaeological team working in the tomb of Vizir Aperia, just beyond the west bank of the Nile. Hidden for five thousand years in a previously unopened burial shaft they found the embalmed and intertwined bodies of two female cats, Etak and Tikk. What was so exciting for professor Peter Sivinty and his team was not the unusually ornate bronze and gold pendants that adorned their necks, nor the remarkable state of preservation of their nonmummified remains, but the fact that between the forelegs of each animal was a carefully rolled funerary papyrus containing the clearly visible marks of a cat's paw. These are the earliest known paintings by a domestic cat and the first conclusive evidence that cat-marking behavior was

LEFT: The Aperia cats (Etak left), holding scrolls, c. 3000 BC. Phakat Museum, Cairo.

known to the ancient Egyptians and considered by them to be of spiritual and aesthetic significance.

The discovery of the Aperia cats led to the immediate reexamination of other feline remains in museums around the world and resulted in a number of other funerary scrolls being found to contain barely discernible paw prints. Where these had previously been noticed they were usually dismissed as dirt or, in one descriptive paper from the Cairo Museum, as "single vertical smear of excess embalming oil."

But why were these paintings made up of only one or two strokes compared to the more complex paintings of today's domestic cats? A likely explanation is that as cats were regarded as the medium through which the gods expressed themselves on Earth, it would have been seen as inappropriate for them to make a confusion of marks. What was required by the priesthood was a simple, unequivocal mark of authority.

RIGHT: The Xois scroll, c. 5000 BC. George Young Museum, Berkeley.

Here the mark of the curious tail has been painted and then negated by a diagonal—a sign from the gods that could be interpreted as an approval to curtail a certain line of inquiry.

RIGHT: The Xois cat, c. 5000 BC. George Young Museum, Berkeley.

This young, unnamed female discovered in the tomb of Nestpeheran on the island of Xois, is shown here as she was found, clutching the Xois funerary scroll (previous page). In keeping with the scroll's message, the cat's tail itself has been arranged in the questioning form, with the tip ending on the eye, which represents the usual dot or paw print that completes this symbol.

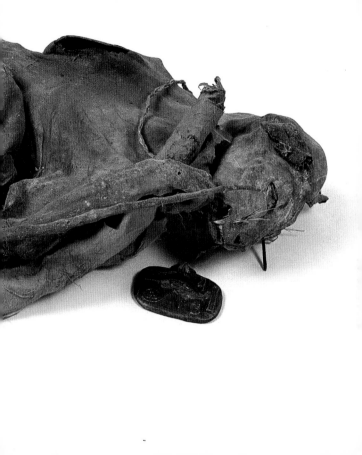

LEFT: A reproduction of the famous tomb wall painting at Deir el–Medina, c. 1250 BC.

Here the sun god Ra in the form of a cat completes what is almost certainly the sign of the curled-over tail and paw dot. This signifies spiritual inquiry and perception of the inner world. The work provides clear evidence that cats' marks were applied as a seal of approval since this cat's painting affirms the hieroglyphics below, which propose that inner perceptions are better confirmed by two cats rather than one.

An explanation of the hieroglyphic symbols that appear under the cat's paw is given on the following pages.

a.

The *udjat* represents the all-seeing eye, which can penetrate the higher spiritual realms that are unavailable to human beings. This symbol is often connected with the cat and can be seen in various forms on the scrolls and pendants shown on previous pages. Note that the eye of the painting cat is in the form of the *udjat*.

b.

This grouping of symbols represents the *ebut*, the painting apparatus used by the cat. The two rounded shapes stand for two different colors of paint. To the left of them, the L-shaped symbol represents the combined easel and paint tray, or *lex*. Underneath is the stool, or *poot,* on which the cat sits while painting. The *ebut* signifies the means of affirmation.

c.

This is the *punkut*, which incorporates the dual sign of the curled-over tail above the oval symbol of *ru*. *Ru* represents the cat's inner eye, doorway to the spiritual realms. The *punkut* stands for the counterbalanced psychic perceptions of two cats, a kind of yin yang of spiritual inquiry.

d.

This almost totally obscured symbol is the *nildjat,* or "the contemplative cat who sits peering into the hidden realms of the spirit world." The *nildjat* represents the triangular form of the cat when seated in the contemplative position with the tail held in the inquiring mode.

It seems most likely then, that once the cat had made its first one or two strokes, it would be considered to have finished and the scroll would have been removed. This view is supported by the Lapis Lazuli funerary scroll (left), where the cat is shown making a very bold paw stroke with great confidence from a position directly above the *udjat*, symbol of the all-seeing eye. Cats with their paws raised were always thought to be making the sign of Ra, god of the sun, but it is now clear that they are painting, and the image of a painting cat is generally recognized to be a sign of celestial approval for the inscriptions on the scroll.

This can clearly be seen in the Xois scroll (page 19), where we read, "free us from the burden of questions, our trust goes forth without questions." Given that the curious form of the tail is so clearly represented in the cat's painting and then negated by a diagonal, it is argued that these words are too appropriate not to have been added later.

LEFT: Funerary papyrus of the Lapis Lazuli cat, c. 5000 BC. Bodhead Library, Oxford.

Note the upright tail position of the painting cat, signifying its pleasure and therefore approval of the hieroglyphic text.

There is little recorded evidence of cats marking between 1000 BC and the Victorian era, other than a few examples during the Middle Ages when cats became associated with witchcraft and were killed by the thousands. Throughout history, cat behavior has been interpreted according to the beliefs current at the time, so once cats fell from favor their scratch marks and paintings, instead of being seen as messages from the gods, were taken as signs of the devil.

We find a graphic example of this in an illustration on an early German story card (right). Here we see the White Queen with her arm draped lovingly around the cat, Betrug, who is making marks on her robe with his paws. The medieval artist has left us in no doubt as to Betrug's character. His piercing eyes and piglike nose give him a grotesquely evil demeanor, and in this old folktale he uses her rouge to mark out a false plan of a vast stone labyrinth so that she will become lost and trapped in its vast corridors.

RIGHT: German story card depicting the White Queen and the wicked cat, Betrug, c. 1430 AD. Katzen-Kunst-Museum, Stuttgart.

Left: *Santo Gato or Didymus,* c. 900 AD. Detail of original, 33 x 24 cm, from *The Book of Kells,* p. 48, chapter 17, St. John's Gospel (St. Columbkille's manuscript). University of Belfast.

A rare case of cat painting being seen in a positive light during the Middle Ages occurs in *The Book of Kells,* where we find an illustration of a saint with the head and paws of a cat. It seems likely that this is Santo Gato (Saint Cat), referred to by Giraldus Cambrensis in his *Topographia Hiberniae,* where he records the legend of a cat who "had many toes and did ably assist with the work of illumination." The cat in *The Book of Kells* does have extra toes (polydactylism), and it is probable that this oddity in one of the monastery cats, coupled with an ability to mark, would have led to its being venerated as a messenger of God.

Overleaf: Medieval bestiary illustration, c. 950 AD. 41 x 27cm. From a manuscript in the Bodhead Library, Oxford.

The cat standing at the easel has taken paint from the conical containers below and is probably drawing a plan of the method to be used to transmute the caged bird and the sleeping dog, prey and enemy of the cat, into gold. Such depictions of the cat involved in experimentally dangerous pastimes doubtlessly led to the expression "Curiosity killed the cat."

By the early nineteenth century, cats were popular in the lounges of well-to-do ladies, and their marking behavior was encouraged as a source of idle amusement. Bowls of flour were provided for cats to dip their paws into and the marks they made were used to fortell the future. Further evidence that cat-marking behavior has been observed for many centuries can be found in several tarot card illustrations. In the Moon card (right), two cats are depicted scooping up the golden waters of the unconscious and using it as a painting medium.

RIGHT: The Moon and the High Priestess tarot cards, c. 1924, from the Cat's Tail tarot, Oracle Deck.

Both of these cards show marks cats have made with their paws and attribute spiritual values to them. In the Moon card, the cat is using the ever-flowing waters of the unconscious as a medium with which to paint flaming cats' eyes to guide us on our journey to enlightenment. The High Priestess appears in the form of a cat, and her marks are given equal weight with the human signs that appear on the twin pillars of wisdom. She has curved her tail into the shape of the horn opposite, so as to present two horns, above which she sits in order to imply a dilemma.

LEFT: Tapestry cushion, c. 1856. 36 x 46 cm. Mary Morris Collection, Ascot.

Amongst the well-to-do in the mid-nineteenth century, cats were encouraged to make marks with flour on velvet cushions, which were then read in much the same way as tea leaves are today. This practice led to the making of cushions especially for the task with appropriate tapestry designs of cats painting. The following well-known children's rhyme also owes its genesis to this pastime.

Pussicat, Wussicat, with a white foot,
On a black cushion your spotty mark put.
One dab is a yes and two is a no,
Pussicat, Wussicat, give us a show.

As of the late nineteenth century, the cat had largely lost its association with the psychic and had become a source of interest to breeders as a pet. Its ability to paint was now treated as a curiosity to be exploited for money rather than studied for any deeper motive. In 1893, a general storekeeper in the village of Otaru, in the north of Japan, sold paintings done by his cat, Otakki, that were vaguely reminiscent of Japanese calligraphic characters. Because of this similarity, he was able to give them a fortune-telling function and use this to attract customers to his store. Stories of Otakki's ability and the wealth she brought her owner spread quickly throughout the country, and by the turn of the century, pictures of her painting had become a symbol of good service and economic success. Even

RIGHT: *Otakki Painting*, 1901. Watercolor on rice paper, 18 x 26 cm. Private collection.

Otakki became famous around the turn of the century for her paintings, which brought many customers to her owner's store in the north of Japan. Statues of cats painting, called *Maneki Neko*, are still put in shop windows throughout Japan as a sign of good service.

today, many shops in Japan have a statue of a cat in the window with its paw raised in the painting position in order to attract customers.

The best-known painting cat in recent history was undoubtedly Mattisa, a ginger tabby who was the star attraction in Mrs. Broadmoore's show in the late 1880s. Mrs. Broadmoore was, in fact, a rather portly gentleman by the name of James Blackmun who did a wicked impersonation of a rather stupid upper-class matron. If the audience came expecting a serious performance as the poster (left) promised, they were evidently not disappointed to be treated instead to a comic act in which Mrs. Broadmoore claimed that the marks made by the cat were in fact pawtraits of people in the audience.

LEFT: *Mrs. Broadmoore's Amazing Painting Cat,* c. 1887. Lithograph, 65 x 47.5 cm. Museum of Animal Acts, Madison.

Cat-marking behavior was trivialized in Victorian times, as this poster shows. While Mattisa certainly painted, most of the performance was concerned with putting down women who might take cat marks seriously rather than encouraging any insight into what the cat's motivation might be.

THEORIES OF FELINE MARKING BEHAVIOR

Biologists are reluctant to concede that cat painting could be aesthetically motivated, preferring instead to explain it either as a form of instinctive territorial marking behavior, or as the playful release of nervous energy. Those holding this latter view cite the abandoned manner in which some cats pounce at the canvas, allowing paint to fly in all directions, as evidence of what is no more than obsessive-compulsive play activity resulting in randomized marks with no meaning whatever. However, to be consistent in this line of reasoning would require us to reject a good deal of human Action Painting as well. The work of Jackson Pollock, Willem de Kooning, and many other Abstract Expressionists could be dismissed on similar grounds.

Most biologists argue that cat painting is merely an extension of the vertical marking activity cats use to demarcate their territory. They claim cats are stimulated to mark by the odor of ammonia salts used as a drying agent in acrylic paints (cats will not paint with oils), which smells remarkably similar to their urine. However, while it is reasonable to assume that the cat's instinctive need to mark its territory may have laid the foundations for its painting behavior, the major reason cats paint today appears to be aesthetic.

We shall never know the origin of the primal feline aesthetic gesture, but it seems that wherever domestic cats are well looked after and have little need to define their territories, their marking behavior tends, in some rare instances, to become what Desmond Morris calls a self-rewarding activity. These activities, "unlike most patterns of animal behavior, are performed for their

---

RIGHT & PAGE 42: Cats not only rely on the scent of their feces to demarcate their territory but also physically mark its position by carefully drawing lines that point toward them like a large arrowhead. These are clearly visible to other cats long after the scent has faded. Sometimes cats use the soil that remains on their paws to make even more visible territorial marks higher up on a tree trunk (right). This type of instinctive vertical marking behavior is thought to have laid the biological foundations for cat painting.

own sake rather than to attain some basic biological goal. They normally occur in animals which have their survival problems under control and have a surplus of nervous energy that seems to require an outlet."

PAGES 46–47: Pinkle, a female Rex, very methodically sorts all the magnetic letters on the refrigerator into color groups. Whether colors have specific meanings for cats is not known, but it is clear they can differentiate between the main color groups and that a few enjoy manipulating them. Attempts to compare this manipulation of ready-made objects to the work of Marcel Duchamp do not stand serious examination.

RIGHT: Pinkle, *Red Letter Day*, 1992. Plastic letters on top of refrigerator, 52 x 78 cm. Photographic collection, Museum of Non-Primate Art, Tokyo.

After forty-five minutes of very slow and careful sorting, Pinkle completes her work by pulling all the red letters onto the top of the refrigerator. This seems to be an entirely self-rewarding activity, for despite encouragement from her owner she will only do it when she wants to, and there appears to be no other reason for her to sort the letters into color groups other than the obvious aesthetic pleasure she derives from it.

But cat painting appears to be motivated by more than the need to release energy and, far from being the result of randomized pawings, is in fact the product of an ability to recognize and manipulate form and structure. For example, we now know that some domestic cats not only are able to distinguish between colors, but seem to enjoy making spatial adjustments to objects of different colors. We also know that some cats that paint representational images often invert them. Nobody has yet come up with a good theory for this behavior, but some contend that the cat is enjoying an exploration of form and structure from a fresh perspective by emphasizing abstract qualities. While biologists are at best skeptical of such a notion, it is interesting to note that the well-known German Neo-Expressionist Georg Baselitz also paints his motifs upside down in order to counteract conventional modes of observation.

While the establishment of a coherent theory of feline marking behavior is still some way off, it has been brought a good deal closer by the work of Dr. Peter Williams, who heads the Department of Applied Aesthetics at Rudkin College in Dallas, Texas. Evidence for an aesthetic motivation was predicated by a series of

BELOW: Studies show that cats spend about 3 percent of their play-hunting time lying on their backs looking at things upside down. A recent theory contends that this may be partly why cats invert objects when they represent them in their paintings. This practice is known as "invertism" and was not discovered until recently because cat representations are very basic and not as easy to recognize when inverted as more complex motifs are.

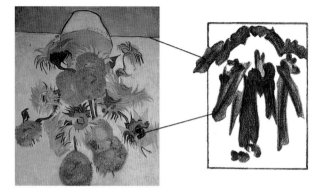

ABOVE & RIGHT: Buster's representation of Van Gogh's *Sunflowers* is a good example of invertism. From a purely visual perspective, the brown mark at the top of the work clearly represents the dark line that defines the edge of the table and the bottom of the vase, as shown in the photograph (left), while the blue marks represent the flowers.

However, biologists interpret these blue marks as territorial and similar in function to the arrowhead paw marks cats make to demarcate their feces. In the painting, these marks signify ownership of the inverted object and are thought to have the function of rendering its unfamiliarity safe.

experiments he ran in 1987 to determine the degree to which domestic cats may display partiality for different works of human art. Because cats show a distinct preference for the works of Van Gogh, usually attributed to their being able to relate to the swirling furlike nature of the brushstrokes, Williams chose four posters of this artist's work and set them low on the wall in the cats' living space. By measuring the amount of time each cat spent looking at the different pictures over a six-week period, he hoped to be able to determine any preferences. However, what he discovered by swapping the positions of the posters around was that, rather than preferring a particular painting, the cats had preferred sitting positions in the room. He called these positions "points of harmonic resonance" because they seemed

LEFT: It appears that cats may be stimulated to paint by localized low energy force fields known as "points of harmonic resonance." Despite his close proximity to Van Gogh's *Sunflowers*, this cat was probably far more inspired by a resonant vibration than by the human artwork, to which its painting bears little relation.

LEFT: The typical pose of a cat when sitting at a point of harmonic resonance. The eyes are slightly closed, and the cat will generally purr and may rock gently back and forth. Almost all cats that paint spend at least ten minutes in resonance prior to commencing a work, which suggests they derive inspirational power from some invisible low-frequency force field. Preferred sitting areas seem to have little to do with warmth, scent, or territorial observation. A cat will simply stop in the middle of nowhere and start purring as if it's just been struck by the most delightful idea.

to be areas where the cat experienced a kind of local-ized force field. He noted that cats spent a large amount of time purring in these places prior to painting and has theorized that some kind of force field, detectable only to cats, may trigger the feline aesthetic response.

Could this be what inspires cats to paint, or do they paint its power? More importantly perhaps, could it be the influence of some intersection of ley lines or some yet-to-be-discovered force field that causes us to see something in a certain way and make us want to paint it? It seems there may be much we can learn about the art of human beings by studying the art of the cat.

RIGHT: The fact that cats spend more time in our company than they do with their own species suggests that there is something in their nature that echoes the higher levels of the human psyche.

FIFTEEN MAJOR ARTISTS

Because this book is designed to function both as a work of reference and as an introduction to contemporary cat painting, it has been necessary to select only those artists who, in the author's opinion, best represent the major movements current at this time. Naturally this has necessitated some omissions, and readers may be surprised to find that several cats whose work has risen to prominence of late are not included. This is usually because their notoriety is based on some particularly unusual technique or performance ability and is not representative of a movement or art style as a whole. Also omitted is a quite recent trend known variously as Fat Cat Chat, Claw Whore, or Neo-Felinistine. Time will tell if this peculiarly violent and destructive form of painting, popularized by the British and American Shorthairs, develops an integrity and viewpoint that would justify its inclusion in a future survey of this kind.

It seems likely as interest in cat painting grows, especially in the newly "awakened" areas of eastern Europe, Russia, and China, that many more feline artists will emerge with entirely new styles and messages. For this reason, we cannot claim that the works included in this selection are representative of cat painting internationally. Rather, they show the important work of a small minority who are currently exhibiting and having their work sold in the West.

Almost all the works in this chapter have been given a title either by the cat's owner or its curator. The reason for this is straightforward. Just as surrounding a painting with an expensive frame and hanging it in a gallery places a value on it, so too, naming a work confirms artistic intent and allows it to be legitimated and taken seriously. Certainly, by titling a cat's painting, we provide a context within which judgments of aesthetic worth are made. A title such as *Fluff and Kittens*, for example, is likely to suggest a different level of worth compared to *Maternal Arrangements* or *Coital Consequences #4*.

Be that as it may, titles nevertheless provide a clue, a starting point, no matter how arbitrary or contextually biased, from which to begin our journey of discovery. Without them, we run the risk of dismissing cat painting as being no more relevant than the mindless territorial daubing of the graffitist.

WONG WONG AND LU LU
Duo Painters

Wong Wong and Lu Lu have painted together for more than ten years. Their initial collaborative works, *Breakfast for Dogs* and *Purr Balls*, 1990, lacked any clear direction. At over five meters long (down both sides of a Fiat Tempra station wagon), these murals were perhaps too ambitious. They lacked spontaneity, and Lu Lu's deft paw strokes were often confused by Wong Wong's exuberant introduction of irrelevant and poorly inverted material from unrelated experiences. While this added to the immediate lightness of the works, it tended to hinder their overall meaning—a far cry from their recent work, *Wollop*, 2001, the name signifying a deeper, more profound relationship and a unity of aesthetic purpose.

LEFT: Wong Wong (top) and Lu Lu, at the Esposizione dell'Arte Felino in Milan. They were selected as guests of the president and jointly won the Zampa d'Oro (Golden Paw) award in 1992.

LEFT: In *Journey by See*, 1992, painted over five days on a brown fence, Wong Wong and Lu Lu's two styles find a satisfying confluence. The finely ridged, even grain of the painted wood reflects the light in web-thin strips that create a microcosm of silken threads, immediately recognizable as the sheen of Wong Wong's rich brown fur. The gaps (small), between the palings (broad), suggest gaps in both experience and collaboration, but triumphantly bridged by joyous shapes and colors that flow from board to board in a continuous, reuniting dance of harmonic bliss.

65

BELOW & PAGE 69: *Galloping*, detail, 1993. Scented acrylic on corrugated iron, 487 x 92 cm. Correa Collection, Madrid.

RIGHT: Interpretive diagram, by Dr. L. P. Ashmead, for *Journal of Applied Aesthetics*, Vol. IV, 1993.
1 & 4: Riding forms

2: Bucking form
3: Grazing form
5: Butterfly (see detail on page 69)
6: Rearing form
7, 8 & 10: Subsidiary shadow forms
9: Leaping form
11: Limb
12: Signatory mark (Wong Wong)

Over the years, Wong Wong and Lu Lu developed a close association with two horses. On cold mornings, the cats would venture out across the fields and spring up onto the generous rumps of their quietly grazing horses. There they'd perch, receiving and imparting warmth. They celebrated this relationship in *Galloping*, 1993 (page 66), painted on a green fence. Here, white and black arched forms appear to gallop together over the regular, green hill-like undulations of the corrugated iron. Lu Lu's delicate bursts of red and yellow overlie and complement (and correct?) Wong Wong's more gestural, less subtle treatment of the major forms, imbuing them with a sense of delight and movement. We are immediately aware of a surging forward—cats and horses together in a joyously energized cavorting—that sweeps us up and takes us along for the ride.

In recent years, Lu Lu's interest in horses has faded and he now paints pigs to the exclusion of all else.

RIGHT: A touch of the old master. In this detail from *Galloping*, Lu Lu captures the essence of a butterfly in flight with just a few deft flicks of his paw. Later the butterfly is drawn to the likeness of itself and flutters around it.

In this he insists that he paint alone and rejects any offers of collaboration from Wong Wong. His favorite subject is Sporca, a local Calabrese pig whose often unsavory and destructive acts perfectly suit Lu Lu's crudely drawn and garishly colored Neo-Expressionistic style. Canvases and paints are quickly chosen. Whatever surface or color is at hand will do, yet his paintings reach out to us with artless guile and artful candor—banal color harmonies that establish new parameters of porcine offensiveness and brutality tinged with the ridiculous.

LEFT: *Pigging Out*, 2002 (a work in progress). Acrylic on fence, triptych, 105 x 98 cm. Collection of the artist, Bologna.

In a curatorial assessment for the Museum of Non-Primate Art, Bariloche, curator Susan Marples wrote, "Lu Lu's fascination with (and probable distaste of) the interplay between pure animal need (eating) and impure (environmentally unsustainable) petrochemical adhocisim (blue plastic clothes basket) is perfectly expressed in this lively and irreverently witty work that cleverly mocks its own authority. This is a well-articulated example of a Neo-Expressionistic work that steers a subtle path between bucolic punk and technological determinism to heighten our awareness of the reductive role of animals in the rural/industrial context."

PURRTLE
Bio-Interactionalist

On mornings when the sun shines obliquely through the aquarium, Purrtle will sometimes spend several hours exciting the red-cap orandas by flicking his fluffy white tail at them. The more frustrated he becomes, the more he flicks, and the more the fish dart about, until simultaneous bursts of high feline and piscine tail energy are engendered. It is these sessions that are the inevitable precursors to Purrtle's painting.

RIGHT: *Tell Tale Tails #7*, 2003. Scented acrylic paste on black card, 78 x 48 cm. Museum of Non-Primate Art, New York.

Using bold downward stokes, Purrtle perfectly captures the essence of pristine form. As art critic Kevin Casey notes, "Purrtle's solipsism poignantly reflects the feline self encountering itself through the juxtaposition of rapidly waving appendages—each coexisting as reluctant coordinates in a glassed-off virtual reality."

72

PEPPER
Portrait Painter

Pepper was born on a small farm near West Town, New York, in the fall of 1979. Being the only male in a litter of six undoubtedly precipitated a premature sense of his own uniqueness, and that, coupled with an umbili-  cal hernia at birth that required constant attention, set him apart from the rest. As early as five weeks old he showed a tendency to be aloof, spending long periods alone gazing at his reflection in the window and, more often than not, content to sit back and observe rather than join in with his sisters' play activities. His mother, while displaying no artistic ability herself, was nevertheless a very conscientious marker of the litter box, and it seems likely that Pepper's considered style was

LEFT: Pepper will spend up to two hours carefully examining himself in a mirror before commencing a self-portrait.

LEFT: Pepper painting *Reflections #54*, 1988. Acrylic on card, 72 x 48 cm. Private collection.

"The relationship of self to a wider context is the antithesis of Pepper's works in self-image, which are iconographically firmly in the mould of egoistic self-portraiture. What is immediately engaging is the aspect of self-image as represented by this detail of his tabby markings, not as they relate to the labyrinth of wider fur patterns, but set apart in clinical isolation, where examination can be decontextualized and deeply revealing." (*Pott T. Exhibition catalog*, New York, 1990.)

LEFT: Pepper painting *Exposure #14* in his Manhattan studio.

Pepper will often fight with his models during their painting sessions, which his owner once explained as being because "he just loses concentration and takes it out on them." A greater insight into this behavior is given by Dr. D. Reynolds writing in the *Bloomsbury Book of Art* (1992). "His model's provocative pose leads to an internalized polarity that explains the incidence of externalized physical conflict during painting sessions."

79

inherited from her.

Almost all his early work involved self-portraiture, and he would typically spend up to two hours carefully examining aspects of himself in a mirror before commencing. He then worked slowly, his painting seeming to inspire a considered awe, as if he were overpowered by the enormity of each mark he made.

It was not until 1987 that Pepper showed any interest in painting Venus, the silver tabby with whom he shared his apartment, and then it was with an impulsive enthusiasm as though he'd never seen her before. Once she was suitably splayed, Pepper would immediately begin to paint. There was no pausing, and the resulting works were lyrical, every aspect of them exhibiting the undiluted essence of quadruped exposure.

LEFT: *Exposure #14*, 1988. Acrylic on card, 72 x 48 cm. Private collection.

Pepper perfectly captures the essence of Venus's exposed form (see page 79). We immediately see the legs splaying out gaily from their central point of attachment, reaching up with an abandonment and optimism reminiscent of Susan Rothenberg's *Maggie's Cartwheel*, 1981.

SMOKEY
Romantic Ruralist

Cats are the only animals other than human beings that regularly use drugs to heighten their aesthetic sensibilities. Smokey is no exception. His painting sessions are always conducted in a secluded part of the garden and inevitably preceded by at least an hour in the catnip patch. This explains not only the slow, almost ponderous way in which he paints, but also the remarkable depth of his pastoral vision.

LEFT: *Serious Ramifications*, 1992. Acrylic on board, 73 x 62 cm. McGillicuddy Art Gallery, Christchurch.

This study of a ram was originally titled *Ramshackle* by the cat's owner, but the title was later changed curatorially.

Smokey has the ability not only to imbue his bucolic forms with elements of the Romantic but also, more importantly, to maintain their dignity. We see this clearly in one of his best-known works, *Serious Ramifications* (pages 82 and 85). "The first thing you notice about the work," says critic Bevan Island, writing in *Cat Art Today*, "is its bold regularity, its obvious symmetry. Not until later do we see the ram walking. But once we do, the feeling of movement is powerful and immediate. We are able to peer through the confusion of moving limbs from a variety of revealing

perspectives as it strides forward, right to left. Light flickers intriguingly as these oblique pediments divide and redivide, impinging upon the mass of yellow dandelions under hoof which appear to explode (implode?) with the impact."

ABOVE: Smokey can be seen completing *Serious Ramifications* in the garden of his Nelson home on New Zealand's South Island. This study of Rodney, a fifteen-year-old ram (left), was the subject of a good deal of contention when it was purchased with public funds by the McGillicuddy Art Gallery in Christchurch for $6,000 in 1993.

OEDIPUS

Aerial Avianist

Oedipus, a five year-old white non-pedigreed who lives in Seattle, is well-known for her avian interpretations. She has a special affinity for the green parakeets that live in her neighborhood and often spends hours high up in the branches of a large cherry tree observing them at close quarters. This fieldwork engenders a high degree of excitement that results in a vigorous painting style, and her owners ensure that canvas and paints are at the ready when she descends. In this way they are rewarded with a host of intricate paintings that regularly sell for more than $750 each at their local gallery, which holds feline art shows twice a year.

RIGHT: *That Cheeky Peeky Parakeety*, 2005. Scented acrylic on card, 75 x 374 cm. Dr. Brie Mazurek Collection, Berkeley.

MISTY
Formal Expansionist

Misty's popularity as a painter is due mainly to the figurative nature of her images. The elegant, bicolored forms, which sometimes extend up to ten meters in length, are immediately evocative and invite a wide range of projective interpretations. For example, in *A Little Lavish Leaping* (left and overleaf), the cat's owner feels that the work concerns an incident in which her four-year-old son deliberately squirted Misty with the hose from the balcony. To her, each pink area describes the typical arched body of a cat as it leaps to avoid danger, while the long black shape clearly represents the water snaking down from above.

However, art critic Michael Dover prefers to tackle the work from a more useful, functional standpoint and feels that it clearly describes some important aspects of feline leaping strategy. The curved black lines describe the path of the leap itself. It begins with the crouched form of the cat ready to spring in the upper right quadrant and follows it down to the pink impact position below, from which it leaps again to land with outstretched paws in the next position.

Others see a dinosaur galloping to the right, and there are those who favor a squirrel jumping down to the left. We can never be sure just what Misty intended. The important thing is that we don't stop trying to understand.

RIGHT & PAGE 88: *A Little Lavish Leaping*, 1993. Acrylic on card and wall, 120 x 170 cm. Preserved in situ, Toronto.

Misty's paintings are greatly valued for their strong yet ambiguous imagery that, combined with contextual uncertainty, allows for a great richness of interpretation. The power of this sort of cat art lies in its very incomprehensibility, which enables it to provoke and intrigue.

GINGER
Neo-Synthesist

Despite showing early signs of an aesthetic marking ability, Ginger did not paint until she was four. Her wallpaper scratchings had always exhibited a delicacy of line and a marked appreciation of surface texture, but she showed no inclination in those first years to explore the use of marking media. These days she likes to make carefully controlled daubs on the window (sometimes only two or three a day) and gradually build up an image that combines (synthesizes) with the scene outside to create an enlivening multidimensional effect, reminiscent of spring blossoms or brightly colored birds on the wing.

LEFT: *Stripped Bare Birds*, 1992. Acrylic paste on glass, 104 x 150 cm. McCahon Trust, Manchester.

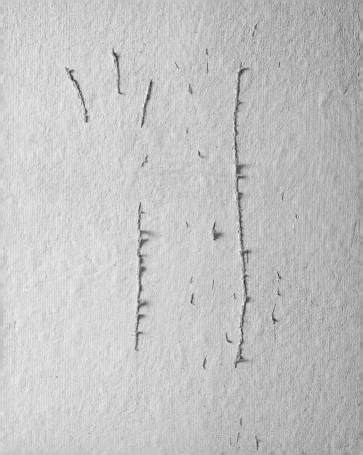

PRINCESS
Elemental Fragmentist

Princess is one of a small number of Elemental Fragmentists, a school of mainly Siamese and Rex painters whose work is typified by an economy of line and form that conveys only the essential elements of just one part, or fragment, of a subject. This is perhaps the hardest of all feline art to understand and the most difficult to recognize in its formative stages. It took two years for her owners to realize that all the elements that characterize her

LEFT: *Amongst the Pigeons*, 1988. Marks with claws on painted fiberboard wall panel, 48 x 72 cm. Private collection.

RIGHT: *Regularly Ridiculed Rodents*, 1993. Ink on paper, 52 x 83 cm. Patrick Hitchings Collection, Perth.

Everything in Princess's work is narrowed to almost totemic simplicity. She often works with an upper and lower canvas, using the lower area for preliminary sketch work before proceeding to the final work above. She usually destroys the lower work, but in some cases prefers it to the upper one, which she will claw down instead.

present style were apparent in the very first scratches she had made as a kitten on her wooden cat door.

In her more classically minimalist works, Princess uses a set ratio of angled-to-vertical strokes (3:2 or 2:3) in a multiplicity of combinations that enable her to explore a wide variety of subjects evoking a rich variation of interpretation. We see this clearly in *Regularly Ridiculed Rodents* (left), which has been variously interpreted as depicting two ostracized rats, the essence of cockroach, a functional detail of her paint roller, and, as one would expect, a host of black magic symbols. Whatever the interpretation, there can be no doubt that Princess, the cat and the painter, manifests a curiously intense subjectivity, a critical awareness of being both the receiver of energy and its translator.

OVERLEAF: *Bounding,* 1991. Diluted ink on paper, 64 x 48 cm. Museum of Non-Primate Art, Tokyo.

Princess focuses on the green tag hanging from Boris's collar. The repetition of green dabs and streaks amongst the light brown verticals (which must represent the dog's fur), gives an immediate sense of the tag flicking about as the dog moves, thus capturing the essential nature of mindless canine cavorting.

CHARLIE
Peripheral Realist

Charlie, who lives in Sydney, Australia, does all his painting on the refrigerator, where the smooth white surface allows him to spread the paint quickly and achieve a lively spontaneity.

Cats use their peripheral vision far more than we realize. This is why they will suddenly look intently in one direction when there seems to us to be nothing there at all. What they are doing is using their more color- and movement-specific peripheral vision to study objects by looking sideways at them. Charlie has just completed an impressionistic work in which the dishtowel appears as a major motif (left) and he can be seen checking his subject peripherally.

LEFT: *The Wild Side*, 1991. Acrylic on enamel, 63 x 101 cm. Collection of the artist.

BOOTSIE
Trans-Expressionist

To watch Bootsie paint is pure delight. As soon as the easel is put up and the paints are laid out next to it, any hint of feline disdain, any trace of detached hauteur, vanishes completely. He almost pounces on the paint, as if he must trap its fleeting vibrance before it escapes, and the moment it is on his paw he springs up to apply it. Consideration appears minimized, while concentration is intense and the strokes are vigorously rhythmical. There is also an obvious intent to lose (loose) self in the work, not holding on to a conscious design, but repeating the strokes as a rhythm, often accompanied by purring, which is common among cats who use a high degree of engagement with bodily process while painting.

LEFT: Bootsie uses a vigorous, sometimes aggressive style to explore his inner feelings and perceptions. He won the Zampa d'Oro (Golden Paw) award at the Esposizione dell'Arte Felino in Milan in 1993 and was runner-up in 1992.

LEFT: *Cross-Purpose Canine*, 2006. Acrylic on cards, 120 x 170 cm. Ata Rangi Crimson Collection, Martinborough.

Bootsie's popularity as a portrait painter is mainly due to the figurative nature of his paintings and his attention to detail and color. He goes to great lengths to examine his animal subjects from all angles and has a decidedly punitive inspection style that ensures his models maintain the poses he chooses for them no matter how uncomfortable.

Equally, he may yowl menacingly at the canvas, then suddenly attack it with a quick stroke of paint and spring away as if, in that one decisive action, he had somehow breathed life into an evil force—created a monster that could reach out and grab him by the paw.

The vitality of image that results from this vigorous style can be clearly seen in *Parrot Time* (right). Art critic Alfred Auty describes it as "a poignant expression of nature's inherent dichotomies [where] one is immediately caught up in the primal duality of fight and flight. Slightly angled, slightly curved strokes are laid close together with perfectly controlled flicks of the paw that at once suggest a frenzy of fluttering feathers, leaping upward, spreading outward; wing(s) beating—Color! Light! Life! Liberty-within-reach—almost!"

RIGHT: *Parrot Time*, 1992. Acrylic on card, 75 x 72 cm. Dr. Philip Wood Collection, Berkeley.

OVERLEAF: Bootsie in full flight during the painting of *Hands Up! Mr. Rooster*, which sold for $15,000. Note the rough sketch he made for this work on the back of the canvas.

TIGER
Spontaneous Reductionist

 The first thing one notices about Tiger's work is its unusual complexity. His multiplicity of colors, intricacy of line, and constant variation of stroke angle to create texture result in paintings with a density of image unique among contemporary cat artists. However, for him art is not the reproduction of reality, but rather reality discovered through its reduction, making his work more controversial than that of most other cats.

As humans, we cannot fail to relate to its delightful complexity of shapes and colors, but equally we are puzzled, even appalled, at Tiger's sudden destruction of it. In order to discover its message, we may need to adopt the cat's mode of concentrated vision and stare directly into the void left by the removal of the painting's center, thus allowing the remaining form that surrounds it to enter our consciousness peripherally.

ABOVE: Tiger working on *Breakfast*, 1991. Acrylic and marking powder on card and wall, 184 x 86 cm. Private collection.

Unlike other feline Reductionists and Neo-Reductionists, such as Puschelchen in Stuttgart and Miezekatze in Cologne, who express the reduced image directly onto the canvas, Tiger's method relies on the reduction of the completed work to the essence of its outer form.

MINNIE
Abstract Expressionist

Minnie (Minnie Monet Manet) spends a good deal of time contemplating amongst the vines before beginning a painting. After a two-year caesura following poor reviews in 1998 and 1999, she now paints as often as once a week.

As soon as Minnie left Lyon and went to live at the little vineyard in Aix-en-Provence, her paintings changed dramatically, and so did the reviews. In 1988, Paul Seuphor had this to say about one of her paintings, titled *Three Blind Mice*. "Three dreary monochromatic daubs with

---

LEFT: *Reindeer in Provence*, 1992. Acrylic on gold card and black wall, 120 x 180 cm. Collection of the artist.

single trickles of excess paint running from each of them are evidently meant to represent blind mice. Certainly, they have no eyes. Nor do they have ears, or legs, or whiskers, or anything else at all except tails. Maybe one can forgive them their difference, but where is their life? Where is the action? Where is the farmer's wife with her big knife? We could definitely do with her to finish off these pathetically uninteresting little blobs of gray." Compare that to the review she received three years later for an exhibition of her

paintings in Arles: "Her work emits a luminosity that cries out with exhilaration, mystery, and revelation. . . . Her many colors and directions allow us to glimpse the inner feline reality."

ABOVE & LEFT: Minnie working on *Reindeer in Provence*. She paints with a pixielike vigor, and the final result often evokes the figurative essence of process as in the work above, which is reminiscent of the "flying" feline form, displaying a flurried orchestration of outstretched limbs. Equally, it may be interpreted along antlerian lines as its human title suggests.

MANKY
Abstract Taxonomist

Manky is a secretive cat and rather unattractive. She likes to hunt, eschews the company of humans, and always paints outside and alone. Where other cats often rely on their "friendliness" to promote their work, Manky's art must sell  entirely on its own merits. And sell it does. Her landscapes are greatly sought after as much for their white serenity as for their interesting infusion of prey. Birds, frogs, rats, mice, voles, and even tiny insects, often decapitated, inhabit large areas of white space so that the resulting works confront us with a disturbing passive-aggressive equilibrium that challenges the great feline myth—that cats enjoy sporting with their prey.

LEFT: *Heads You Lose, Tails I Win*, 2005. Scented acrylic on card 98 x 78 cm. Dr. Lois Mills, Kansas City.

RUSTY

Psychometric Impressionist

Psychometric Impressionism involves the creation of images which reflect not the appearance of a particular object, but rather the situations or locations the object has been involved with in the past. In order to create such a work, the  cat artist will spend a good deal of time sniffing, patting, and rubbing against the object or animal whose psychometric impression it wants to convey before it commences its painting. Because of their psychic abilities, cats are highly adept at this form of expression and

---

LEFT: *Blue Bike Blues*, 1990. Scented acrylic on glass, 98 x 78 cm. Dr. Pat Morris Trust, Ascot.

Rusty prefers to work on glass so he can keep in constant touch with the object and allow the essence of its significant past to pervade his sensibilities as he paints.

Rusty, an Abyssinian who hails from Edinburgh, is one of the world's leading exponents of the art.

Rusty's choice of subject matter is contingent upon whether it has some special significance for him, and this is the aspect he expresses in his paintings. In *Blue Bike Blues* for example (page 118), he chose a bicycle that a child had used to run over his tail the day before. In his inverted psychometric impression of a Russian doll (right, situated in bottom left corner), Rusty applied acrylic powder to the condensation on the window and then added further detail by scratching the dried paint. Prior to painting, he had played with all five progressively smaller dolls contained within the larger one, and he watched carefully when his owner put them all together again. His later prolonged attempts to "reach" the other smaller dolls clearly had a profound psychometric effect on him, as evidenced by the fractured nature of the work and the little scratch marks he made in the paint, which suggest an attempt to find a way inside.

***

RIGHT: *Russian Doll*, 1990 (work in progress). Acrylic powder on glass, 120 x 180 cm. Photo courtesy of centre de recherche dans les arts graphiques félins, Paris.

OTHER FORMS OF ARTISTIC EXPRESSION

The number of domestic cats actively painting in the world today is minuscule, maybe a few hundred at the very most out of the estimated two hundred million currently living with human beings. There are, however, many more hundreds of cats who use other forms of artistic expression, and no survey of this kind would be complete without some reference to them.

The use of upholstery by cats has only recently been recognized as an important area of feline aesthetics. While the techniques used in these works may look simple enough, the older, less flexible fabrics and coarse horsehair stuffings involve considerable modelling

---

LEFT: Maxwell with *Gerty*, a work in progress. Clever use of negative space between the loosened brocade and its upper support implies an open mouth, and the whole work (including the legs) almost certainly portrays the frontal aspect of Gertrude, the Saint Bernard dog with whom Maxwell shares his home.

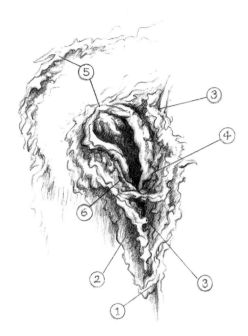

Above: Constructional diagram by Anne Hindry. The numbers refer to the amount of time (in weeks) the cat has taken over each section.

ABOVE: Maxwell, *Opening*, 1992. Appropriated red couch, 68 x 37 x 9 cm. Collection of the artist.

When this piece by Maxwell (page 122) was first exhibited in 1993, it received great praise from art critic Gertrude Greer, who saw it as "a very exciting, obviously invertist work and certainly more powerful than his later painted images with their rather boring predominance of phallocentric verticals."

problems, and some cats have to resort to binding fibers together excrementally or adding the required textural interest with salivary excretions. Owing almost entirely to owner ignorance, many cats are not given access to paints at this stage and forced to continue with soft sculpture. For cat artists, the increasing use of furniture made of easily worked synthetic materials and degradable yet coherent foams has, on the surface, been beneficial. But these modern mediums are not without their problems, and it is now becoming difficult to distinguish between serious attempts to develop new signs that make full use of the feline aesthetic and what one art critic describes as "the merely dilettantish reliance on the occasional dramatic effect."

While aesthetic clawing is a relatively common feline creative technique, one must be careful to distinguish between the irrelevant and destructive scratchings that are occasionally exhibited by ignorant owners in the hope of financial gain and those scratch-forms that demonstrate a high degree of considered artistic intent.

OPPOSITE PAGE, LEFT: Bonny, *Come On In*, 1990. Appropriated lounge chair, 92 x 89 x 78 cm. Private collection.

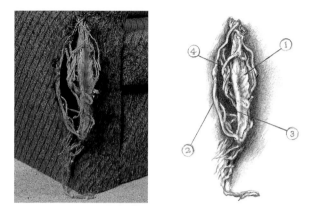

ABOVE, RIGHT: Interpretive diagram by Tom Scott:
(1) tail form; (2) erogenous edging; (3) ovoidal aperture;
(4) restrictive vine forms. Writing about this work in an
exhibition catalog of the Gallery of Non-Primate Art,
Philadelphia, Peter Muxlew said, "The synthetic fiber has
been carefully frayed to resemble the texture and color of a
cat's tail in the upright welcoming position—inviting, yet
guarding the entrance beyond. However, this controlling tail
is itself compromised by restrictive vines so that the whole
erogenously edged aperture hints at pleasure tinged with the
possibility of entanglement."

There can be little doubt of this when the work has taken a long time to complete, especially in the case of a chewing or mouth sculpture, which is usually the product of great dedication by a cat with a determined sense of purpose. *Bad Cat* (left), by Fritz from Los Angeles, falls into this category.

What immediately strikes the eye is the bold use of negative space to create the image of a cat (tail upright, front leg forward) walking straight toward us—striding defiantly through this mean, light-slitting, mass-produced technobarrier that curls back as if melted by searing heat. Fritz is not swayed by any promptings of feline Zeitgeist, and while his work arguably borders on Avant-Grunge with its celebration of second-degree white trash, it nevertheless brings into focus the

---

LEFT: *Bad Cat*, 1991. Appropriated venetian blinds, 114 x 167 cm. Rosemarie Trickel Trust, Berkeley.

It required nine months of diligent gnawing and clawing by Fritz to create this bold image of a cat searing its way through a domestic technobarrier. The work clearly alludes to the constraining effect of mass-produced products on the contemporary cat's freedom of movement.

artist's serious concern with the confining effects of modern technology on the domestic cat. Fritz's death in 1993 (electrocuted while completing a Reconstructionist sculpture on a TV cord), was a great loss to the movement, but he leaves behind an impressive oeuvre, including his well-known Barbie chewings *The Zen of Ken*, 1991, and *The Sound of One Leg Flapping*, 1992.

Marking on a very hard substance like metal (right), provided it is done over a long period and in compliance with the two natural laws that govern effective territorial signing, can also initiate an aesthetic sense. To be powerful, a territorial mark must first be repeated as often as possible in the most highly populated areas so it becomes widely known amongst a given population of cats. Secondly, it must be distinctive yet still easily recognizable as a territorial demarcation. A cat using such a mark in this way will be rewarded with a well-secured territory. Each time it makes its special mark, each time it sees it, the cat feels secure and is encouraged to repeat the process. Gradually, the artist becomes better at it, is able to do it more quickly, and learns where it is most effective. Eventually, this evolving aesthetic judgment and technical skill may

ABOVE: Fritz with *When the Cat's Away*, 1990. Claw marks on painted metal guttering, 16 x 67 cm. Photo courtesy of the Institute for the Promotion of Cat Art, London.

develop into the ability to make representational marks.

Cats possess an exceptionally flexible skeletal structure and a well-muscled body, which enables them to adopt and hold a large repertoire of poses for long periods of time. Despite this, surprisingly few choose body sculpture as a mode of artistic expression. The few cat owners who insist otherwise often fail to distinguish between their cat's rehearsal of the extremely slow, controlled movements necessary for hunting by stealth and genuine examples of performance art, which involves frozen body positions specifically designed to effect a change in the viewer. These performances are usually put on for the benefit of other cats, and although they may occasionally display for mice and even birds, they seldom bother with dogs, who for some reason become highly agitated and often aggressive when viewing this form of art.

Litter box marking is one of the most common and widely accepted forms of feline art. Cats rely primarily on the scent of their feces and urine to mark their territory, but some will seek to accentuate the position of their deposits in an attempt to ensure that they continue to act as markers long after the scent has faded.

ABOVE: By mimicking the pointy and whiskered nature of a mouse's nose, this cat is able to impress his viewer with an impassioned characterization of the victim position.

OVERLEAF: This cat uses her own body to make a living sculpture of a mouse, thereby creating an empathetic, one-to-one communication between artist and viewer, cat and mouse.

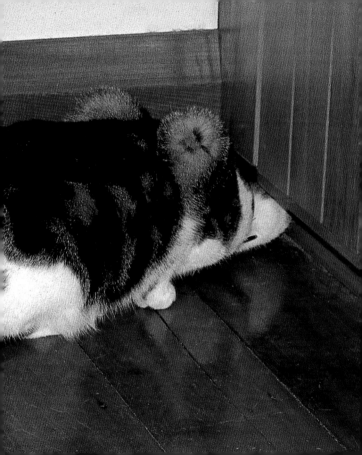

We've all seen how cats do this; carefully scraping long grooves in the earth or litter that point directly to the feces like a broad arrowheads. To further extend this demarcation, some cats will will use the earth or litter that remains on their paws to make even more-visible marks like a signature higher up on a nearby vertical surface, such as a tree trunk or wall. It is this type of instinctive vertical marking behavior that is thought to have laid the biological foundations for cat painting.

If a cat has artistic potential, its litter box signature lines will tend to be quite symetrically placed or may be typified by regular curved forms of varying complexity. Reseach has shown that if a cat spends up to ten minutes a day contemplating its own or others' litter box marks, it is likely to have advanced aesthetic sensibilities.

LEFT: The classic litter box pattern involves two or three deep grooves arrowing toward the feces. Obsessive marking by insecure or oversensitive cats often results in their creating more-decorative lines to accentuate their deposits. This has led to the theory that sensitive cats, like sensitive humans, are more likely to be artistically inclined so as to ensure that their territories are well decorated and therefore demarcated.

Like children, many cats enjoy the ease with which products like shampoo and conditioner can be applied to shiny bathroom surfaces, and this form of marking can often lead to painting with real paints. Of course, unless encouraged to use a more absorbent canvas, their work will lack discipline and their paintings may become simply a therapeutic pastime rather than a serious exploration of their deeper feelings and emotions. Argon's work (right), does not fall into this category. Writing in the *Journal of Cat Art Today*, critic Clive Patton suggested that "Argon's poorly controlled verticals may in reality be designed to boldly obviate (and thereby criticize?) the functionality of the male appendage, which has been clearly rendered in black. Why he should choose to do this is a matter for conjecture, but we have learned from this talented young artist's guardian that he spends a considerable amount of time observing him in the bath, and it may well be that this work is an attempt to contrast his

---

RIGHT: *Untitled*, 1994 (work in progress). Appropriated bath tub, 97 x 78 cm. Photographic collection, Museum of Non-Primate Art, Tokyo.

own (discreet) retromingent style with that of his more forward (arrogant?) human companion. On the other hand, it may be a simple yet cogent comment on the inappropriate nature of (involuntary?) urinary excess in the ablutionary context."

Installations involving dead animals or parts of dead animals have had an unfortunate history of being misunderstood. The human intolerance of rodents in particular, and a revulsion of skinned or plucked animal bodies in general, has resulted in the destruction of many valuable feline works using these forms. Worse still, the numerous cats who choose to express themselves by carefully displaying these valuable tokens of life in the home, where they can best be appreciated and protected, are admonished for their efforts and, as a result, discouraged from pursuing the only line of creative endeavor they know.

By bringing dead, or nearly dead, prey back to the center of their territory, many cats are simply making a

RIGHT: Radar prepares a mouse for one of his nocturnal installations. These sometimes involve the use of stairs to create interesting spatial juxtapositions.

reciprocal gesture—leaving freshly killed food in return for the food they have been given by their owners. However, there is a growing number of cats, both male and female, who reportedly go to great pains to arrange and rearrange these small carcasses or sections of carcasses, with so much care and precision over such a long period of time that the resulting designs can be regarded as none other than well-considered and deeply meaningful forms of artistic expression.

LEFT: Radar, *Infra-mice*, 1994. Temporary installation, lounge carpet, 13 x 12 cm. Santa Monica.

Reviewing this work for *Cat Art Today*, critic John Roberts wrote, "This is a beautifully balanced and peaceful arrangement of two dead mice, who seem to float together on a calm grey ocean. Their tiny bodies, wet and dishevelled, are swept along and seem to merge in a union of spiritual intent. Radar shows a fascination here with the inevitability of separation and the corresponding need to struggle for contact. The problem is how to achieve this without surrendering that deep sense of feline independence the artist must feel in her innermost being."

SELECTED BIBLIOGRAPHY

ARORA, D. "Psychedelicacy: The Effects of Catmint on the Creative Behavior of Domestic Cats." *Cat Art Today*, Vol. II 1992.

BALL, H. 1992. *Paws for Thought: The Magic and Meaning of Litter Tray Relief Patterns.* Slive & Seymour, Cambridge.

COVERT, J. *Alley Art: Bad Cats Do Their Stuff.* Dryfhout Press, New Hampshire.

DENIS, M. 1989. *More Paw Less Claw: Helping Your Cat Develop a Better Technique.* Order Press, New York.

LONG, R. 1990. *Feline Artistic Potential: Stretching Your Cat Creatively.* Knight & Christopher, Los Angeles.

LORD-OSIS, J. "Pawnography: Paw Marking as a Mode of Sexual Communication amongst Domestic Cats in Sweden." *Journal of Applied Aesthetics*, Vol. VI, 1991.

MUTT, R. "Decorative Retromingency: Urinary Embellishment as a Major Problem in the Curation of Feline Art." *Journal of Non-Primate Art*, Vol. XV, 1991. Press, Perth.

WUNDERLICH, R. 1993. *Why Dogs Don't Paint.* Da Costa & Kaufmann, Princeton.

For more information visit **www.monpa.com**